The Harcombe Diet®
Lunch box recipes

Quick, easy and nutritious meals
for busy people on the go

Published by Columbus Publishing Ltd 2014
www.columbuspublishing.co.uk

ISBN 978-1-907797-43-9
Rev 20140802

Cover design by Lewis Kokoc

The content of this book is intended to inform, entertain and provoke your
thinking. This is not intended as medical advice. It may, however, make you
question current medical and nutritional advice. That's your choice. It's your life
and health in your hands. Neither the authors nor the publisher can be held
responsible or liable for any loss or claim arising from the use, or misuse, of the
content of this book.

COLUMBUS PUBLISHING

Contents

The Harcombe Diet®
Lunch box recipes

**Find out more about Zoë and/or
The Harcombe Diet® at:**

www.zoeharcombe.com

www.theharcombediet.com

www.theharcombedietclub.com

Introduction

When we worked in corporate life and travelled extensively, we were shocked by the poor selection of food available to the travelling public, be it motorway service stations, on trains or 'planes.

For the relatively few days that we were office based, we would have lunch in the work canteen, or grab a quick take-out snack from the local 'deli'. The former was a bit like school lunches: pizza; pasta; potatoes; pies and puddings - things beginning with 'P' because they make you 'Porky'! The latter was invariably some baguette-based creation containing a few salad leaves and a slice of tomato.

Today, even with the growth in 'healthy options', the general quality of food on offer for the traveller or corporate worker is shockingly poor.

A day out for a business meeting, or an overseas trip for a holiday, can prove a real challenge for a consumer of real food.

The challenge is even greater for those working in offices and factories and becomes worse still for those having to work unsociable shift patterns.

Meals on the go are still, typically, wheat based produce in the form of a sandwich or pizza with a couple of salad ingredients thrown in to add some colour. They are generally tasteless and do little to nourish our bodies through the day.

Unless you are fortunate to have a work canteen with a proper deli bar, or a local restaurant and a decent budget, making your own packed lunch is the only option for us 'real foodies' who want a decent meal while out and about and at work.

Many of us are happy to throw together some of last night's chilled leftovers into a tub and take it to work. But why compromise? Preparing a delicious lunch box, which makes your mouth water when you lift off the lid and then leaves you nourished and satisfied for the rest of your working day, takes a bit of planning and organising, but it is so worth the effort.

In this handy little book, we'll show you how to do just that.

There's no need to go hungry while out and about. There's no need to grab some tasteless, starchy sandwich on the run. From now on, with just a small amount of planning and preparation, you can have tasty, healthy and nutritious meals on the go.

Chapter 1
About this book

The Harcombe Diet® encourages you to eat as much 'real' food as you need, three times a day. The appendices at the back of this book contain handy reminders of what you can eat in Phase 1, Phase 2 and Phase 3.

Most people reading this book will be familiar with The Harcombe Diet®, so you'll appreciate the "Suitable for" information at the end of each recipe. This will tell you if the recipe is OK for the three conditions, which phase of the diet the recipe is for and whether this is a 'carb' or a 'fat' meal.

For anyone not familiar with the diet, theharcombediet.com site will give you the headlines about the diet, the phases and these all-important conditions, which explain food cravings.

We have tried to include as many Phase 1 options as possible. There are also a lot of fat meals, as we know that it's easier to do brown rice/rice pasta dishes at home. We also know that fat meals are popular among Harcombe followers because we know that fat is our friend!

We've marked vegetarian options (V) on the list of recipes for mains/salads/sauces & dips and in the title for each recipe. A number of the vegetarian options mix real foods (they use seeds and nuts or pulses and cheese, for example). We've included these for two reasons 1) because they are awesome recipes and 2) because we are trying to encourage the mindset that filling up on real food, even with some mixing, is infinitely better than settling for a sandwich with 50 different ingredients.

We work long hours nowadays. Many of you will be having breakfast at 6-7am and not getting home for dinner until 12 hours later. If one great meal in the middle of the day can stop you snacking and having a bad lunch option, the fact that you're mixing is really not a problem.

On this theme, you will find an occasional apricot in a recipe and avocado in a couple. We point out where you can leave things out and where there is a tiny mix (as opposed to a whole recipe mix). Our recommendation is to go with these tiny flexes. The goal is to get you through the day with a super healthy lunch and a wee mix is really not going to hurt.

We've intentionally not included desserts, as you shouldn't need them as part of your lunch box. If you really need something to finish off your meal, have some berries or a square of dark chocolate (at least 70% cocoa and ideally 85% or higher).

The book is structured in three sections:
- Mains
- Salads
- Sauces & Dips

When making your lunchbox for the day, we recommend that you simply add something from each group: a main dish; one, or more salads and a sauce or dip. A perfect Phase 1 combo would be lemon roast chicken with beetroot and watercress salad and herb infused olive oil. Do let us know your favourite combinations in theharcombedietclub.com or on Facebook.

And finally - don't forget the little people! All the recipes in this book are, of course, suitable for children's school lunch boxes too, whatever teacher may say ;-)

Chapter 2
What you'll need

Out and about

You'll need a good range of Tupperware boxes. Most people are likely to have a few in the house already. If not, you'll find everything from half litre to two litre containers handy. Do get a couple of really small ones, under half a litre, as they're great for the sauces and dips. One in the wash and one in use is worth remembering too.

You'll need a set of cutlery that you're happy to carry around with you. Metal is best, but you may also want to have some disposable plastic sets in case you need to take a lunch when you're flying off somewhere.

For the summer months, you may find a small cool bag useful, to keep your food chilled and fresh when you're out and about.

For hot meal options, food flasks are a great invention. If you're someone who prefers hot meals to cold, then invest in a quality food flask. And, of course, they can be used for cold meals too.

At home

We've looked to keep the recipes in this book simple to make and to store, so that you can make them without the need for specialised equipment or ingredients.

In the kitchen you'll need little more than an oven and a blender and a flan tin/baking tray here and there.

There may be a handful of ingredients that need a bit of looking for, but the majority you will be able to find in your local supermarket or grocer, if they are not already in your larder cupboard.

We recommend keeping the following staples at home:

Herbs and spices:
Cayenne pepper, cumin seeds, peppercorns, sea salt, garlic, coriander seeds, mixed herbs, paprika, turmeric, chilli powder.

Larder items:
Olive oil, sesame oil, white wine vinegar, rice flour, almond flour, red/green lentils, balsamic vinegar, Dijon mustard, Harissa paste, Tabasco.

Tinned produce:
Tomatoes, tuna/salmon, kidney beans, chickpeas.

For the fridge:
Bell peppers, mixed lettuce leaves, tomatoes, onions (white and red), Natural Live Yoghurt (NLY), cheddar cheese, butter.

Other staples:
Eggs, mince meat, chicken.

Some preparation time

If you want the quickest and easiest lunch option then just take a tub of salad leaves into work, with some dressing in a separate jar/tub to keep the leaves fresh and then pop some cold meat, a tin of fish or grated cheese on top of the salad at serving time and that's lunch.

This book is about putting in a bit more effort to prepare something really special, so that you feel you've really had a great meal.

We have long encouraged a back-to-baking Sunday. A little time invested in preparing food options on a Sunday, or one evening a week, will transform your lunch options and it can be great fun. All the time we spend watching cookery programmes, we could be doing it ourselves!

Our weekday lunches will, mainly, be a mixture of three or four groups of pre-prepared ingredients and it's these groups of ingredients that will need preparing in advance.

Other recipes will involve pre-cooking, or part-cooking, and chilling or freezing so that a suitable meal portion can be quickly packed and taken to work with you.

Of course, the recipes are not limited to work lunches only. They can form the perfect basis for snacks, picnics or even a quick and easy meal at home. They're also great for an 'as-you-like-it' meal, an ensemble of various dishes laid out on a table for you to enjoy as you please. If you have children, they'll love 'as-you-like-it' meals and you may be surprised at how much even the pickiest of eaters will eat when they have a range of delicious, colourful and healthy foods to select from, especially if you let them eat with their fingers!

For a typical week, where two adults need five lunchboxes, we estimate that the preparation time need be no more than a couple of hours. You'll reduce this further with practice and you can always save time by having a main dish for an evening meal, which you can then use in your lunchbox for the next couple of days. For example, go for a slightly larger than usual pork joint for a slow roast one evening and you'll have leftovers for lunches for the next couple of days.

As with everything in life - you'll get out of this what you put in and we so hope that you enjoy the putting in as much as the getting out and feel encouraged to start and maintain a great lunch box habit.

Chapter 3

Useful notes

When we list weights or volumes for ingredients, these are always pre-cooked weights and volumes. Hence "100g brown rice" on the ingredients list will be 100g of brown rice grains straight from the packet – the weight will approximately double when cooked for this particular ingredient. 200g of spinach, on the contrary, will reduce in weight a little and substantially in volume, when it is cooked.

Most recipes are designed to serve four people. Please adjust the quantities to suit your family size and/or to make some leftovers for another meal.

To make the recipes easy to follow, we have listed all the ingredients in the order that you will use them.

Many of our recipes refer to a large frying pan. This can be a wok – whatever you normally use to fry things with minimal olive oil.

If there is anything you don't like in a recipe, leave it out or swap it for something similar (one spice for another, one vegetable for another etc). Recipes are meant to be adapted to suit your tastes.

Please check any tins or packets for unnecessary ingredients. You'll find sugar in tins of vegetables and pulses unless you're careful. Tins of tomatoes usually have citric acid as an added ingredient – this is fine as a preservative. Stock cubes are virtually impossible to get without sugar (an 'ose') somewhere on the list. Get one with any nasties as far down the list as possible and then don't worry. The cube is usually about a centimetre squared and it ends up being added to a lot of liquid in a dish serving four people, so the amount you end up with is absolutely minute.

Tinned vegetables are fine. Tinned fish is especially healthy, if you choose the options with bones and skin left in - that's where the vitamin D is most concentrated. Frozen vegetables are also fine as an alternative to fresh vegetables and useful to keep in stock.

We always recommend Natural Live Yoghurt (also called bio on some labels) and this is important for Phase 1. For Phase 2 recipes, it's OK to use normal yoghurt, if you can't get live yoghurt.

Weights, measures & temperatures

We've used the metric system for weights and temperatures and have also included an imperial conversion where appropriate.

We list Fahrenheit, Celsius and gas marks on every recipe to make sure that the setting for your own oven is always to hand, without the need to convert.

For completeness, here is a useful reminder of the various conversions that you may need while using this book.

Oven temperature conversions:

Fahrenheit	Centigrade	Gas Mark	Description
225 – 275 f	110 – 135 c	0 – 1	Very Cool
300 – 325 f	150 – 165 c	2 – 3	Cool
350 – 375 f	175 – 190 c	4 – 5	Moderate
400 – 425 f	200 – 220 c	6 – 7	Hot
450 – 475 f	230 – 245 c	8 – 9	Very Hot

Conversion table for weight: Metric to imperial

Metric	Metric	Imperial	Imperial
g	Kg	Oz	Lbs
100	0.1	3.5	0.22
250	0.25	8.75	0.55
500	0.5	17.5	1.1
1000	1	35	2.2

Conversion table for volumes and liquids:

USA	Universal	Imperial	Imperial	Metric	Other
Cups	Tablespoons	Fluid oz	Pints	Ml	
1/16	1			15	= 3 teasp
1/8	2	1		30	
¼	4	2	1/8	60	
½	8	4	¼	120	
¾	12	6	1/6	175	
1	16	8	½	240	
2	32	16	1	480	
4.2	68	34	2.1	1000	= 1 litre

Chapter 4

Mains

This is the 'meaty' chapter, where we look at the delicious recipes that you can be enjoying for your packed lunch as soon as tomorrow (depending on what you have in your fridge right now).

There is no fixed portion size for each main item and you should adjust the quantities to suit what you need to get you through your busy day and to your next complete meal.

We all get times when our blood sugar gets a bit low, we get the shakes and we reach for a snack. Having some healthy snacks available in your fridge or lunchbox helps to make sure that you make good choices for your health, rather than succumbing to a sugar laden cereal bar or bar of confectionery.

Like all the recipes in this book, these dishes can be made in advance and will usually keep for five days or more in a fridge (depending on the original freshness of ingredients).

In this Chapter:

Chicken – Roast, lemon & garlic, herb crusted, mustard, chilli roast
Tandoori chicken
Chicken breast stuffed with Guacamole
Bacon wrapped chicken
Cheese topped chicken breast
Cajun seasoning (For chicken, pork, beef, bacon, fish etc.)
Kebabs - Pork, chicken or beef

Coronation chicken wrap
Chicken burgers
Slow roast pork
Mustard roast ham
Scotch eggs
Zingy fish patties
Chilli prawns
Harissa spiced Koftas
Meatzas
Meatza Toppings - Quattro Stagioni, Margherita, Tex-Mex
Lunchbox 'Eggza' (v)
Homemade pâté
Chicken liver parfait
Cheese & bacon muffins
Loaded bacon strips (with guacamole/salsa)
Egg mayonnaise (v)
Omelette strips (v)
Oopsies (v)
Frittata (v)
Spicy chick pea patties (v)
Wheat free flans (v) – Courgette, pepper & Mozzarella, Roasted tomato & Feta, Asparagus & Cheddar cheese
Lentil & buckwheat biscuits (v)
Lentil & cheese slab (v)
Carrot, parsnip, celeriac & mixed seed bake (v)
Chewy fruit bars (v)
Nut Roast (v)

(v) = vegetarian

Roast chicken

Poulet roti was always one of Andy's favourite meals during the years he lived in France. The moist texture of a slow roast bird, coupled with its deliciously crispy skin, was always a feast to look forward to. And, of course, any leftovers were always a welcome addition to the next day's lunchbox.

We're suggesting a couple of options to the basic roast chicken and, if you follow the same cooking method for them all, you'll end up with the same delicious 'roti'.

1 whole chicken.

Basic method:
1 Pre heat the oven 175° C, 350° F, Gas 4.
2 Wash the chicken inside and out and dab the skin with kitchen roll to dry. Place the bird in a bowl for a few minutes to allow any water to drain away.
3 Place the chicken, breast side down, in a roasting dish and pop in the oven for 30 minutes. This will allow juices to flow into the breast meat, making it lovely and moist.
4 Remove from the oven and carefully turn the bird over, taking care not to puncture the skin. Pop back in the oven and roast for a further 30 minutes.
5 Turn the oven temperature up to 200° C, 400° F, Gas 6 and roast for a further 30 minutes until the skin is a nice crispy brown and the juices run clear.

Portions: 4
Suitable for: Phase 1 & 2 (fat).
Candida, Hypoglycaemia, Wheat free, Dairy free.

Lemon & garlic roast chicken

1 chicken
2 cloves garlic, peeled
1 lemon, cut in quarters.

1 Wash and prepare the chicken as in the basic method.
2 Put the garlic cloves into the chicken and then squeeze the juice of the lemon into the chicken. Pop the remaining wedges in too.
3 Cook as per the basic method.

Portions: 4
Suitable for: Phase 1 & 2 (fat).
Candida, Hypoglycaemia, Wheat free, Dairy free.

Herb crusted chicken

1 chicken
1 onion, peeled and quartered
2 tablespoons olive oil
2 teaspoons dried mixed herbs.

1 Wash and prepare the chicken as in the basic method.
2 Put the onion into the chicken.
3 Rub the olive oil onto the chicken skin and then sprinkle the mixed herbs all over the skin (the olive oil will help the herbs to stick).
4 Cook as per the basic method.

Portions: 4
Suitable for: Phase 1 & 2 (fat).
Candida, Hypoglycaemia, Wheat free, Dairy free.

Mustard roast chicken

Strictly speaking we don't allow mustard in Phase 1, but you have to try this to believe how much difference a scraping of mustard can make to a chicken. You can save this recipe until Phase 2. Or have it in Phase 1 and give the skin (the mustard in effect) to someone else. Or be chilled about the fact that half a teaspoon of mustard (your share in the recipe) will make so little difference that the taste is worth it.

1 chicken
1 onion, peeled and quartered
2 teaspoons Dijon mustard.

1 Wash and prepare the chicken as in the basic method.
2 Put the onion into the chicken.
3 Spoon the mustard over the chicken and, using the back of the spoon, make sure that the breast, legs and wings are evenly covered.
4 Cook as per the basic method.

Portions: 4
Suitable for: Phase 2 (fat).
Candida, Hypoglycaemia, Wheat free, Dairy free.

Chilli roast chicken

1 chicken
2 tablespoons olive oil
2 teaspoons chilli flakes.

1 Wash and prepare the chicken as in the basic method.
2 Rub the olive oil into the chicken skin and then sprinkle
the chilli flakes all over the skin.
3 Cook as per the basic method.

Portions: 4
Suitable for: Phase 1 & 2 (fat).
Candida, Hypoglycaemia, Wheat free, Dairy free.

Tandoori chicken

Tandoori chicken is as delicious cold as it is hot. You can use your favourite piece of chicken - legs, breasts, wings - or cook a whole one and chop it up as required.

4 chicken pieces
200g (7oz) Greek style Natural Live Yoghurt
3 teaspoons tandoori spice mix (1 teaspoon each of ground ginger, ground cumin, ground coriander, paprika, turmeric, salt, cayenne pepper)
Sea salt and freshly ground pepper.

1 Pre-heat the oven to 200° C, 400° F, Gas 6.
2 Slash the chicken pieces and place them in a shallow dish.
3 Thoroughly mix the yoghurt, spices, salt and pepper and pour over the chicken pieces, turning the chicken pieces so that they are well covered. Cover with cling film, chill and leave for at least 8 hrs.
4 Pop the chicken in the oven and roast for about 30 minutes until the chicken is cooked through.
5 Chill and use as required.

Portions: 4
Suitable for: Phase 1 & 2 (fat).
Candida, Hypoglycaemia, Wheat free.

Chicken breast stuffed with Guacamole

Not only does this dish look exotic, it tastes it too. No one, yourself included, will believe you knocked it up in 15 minutes.

4 chicken breasts
4 tablespoons guacamole. (see page 88).

1 Place the chicken breast skin side down on a tray and grill for 5 minutes. Turn the breast over and grill for a further 5 minutes until cooked through and the skin turns brown and crispy. Put aside to cool.
2 When cool, slice along the length of the breast to open up a pouch, into which you can stuff the guacamole.
3 Chill and use as required.

Portions: 4
Suitable for: Phase 2/3 (fat).
Candida, Hypoglycaemia, Wheat free, Dairy free.

Bacon wrapped chicken

This is a really simple way to spruce up a chicken breast, and it just takes 15 minutes to prepare and cook. It's delicious with our raw tomato salsa (page 80).

4 chicken breasts
4 large bacon rashers.

1 Take a chicken breast and tightly wrap a bacon rasher around it. Pierce with a cocktail stick to hold in place. Repeat for the other 3 breasts.
2 Place the chicken pieces on a tray and grill for 5 minutes. Turn the breasts over and grill for a further 5 minutes until cooked through and until the bacon fat is nice and crispy.
3 Chill and use as required.

Portions: 4
Suitable for: Phase 1 & 2 (fat).
Candida, Hypoglycaemia, Wheat free, Dairy free.

Cheese topped chicken breast

This recipe uses chicken as a base for a classic dish (rather than toast). Like the bacon wrapped chicken, this is delicious with our raw tomato salsa (page 80).

4 chicken breasts
50g (2oz) grated cheddar (or similar hard cheese).

1 Take a chicken breast and slice it along its length, leaving just enough meat to hold it together as a single breast. Place it on a chopping board and lightly bash it with your fist until flat. Repeat for the other breasts.
2 Place the chicken pieces on a tray and grill for 5 minutes. Turn the breasts over and grill for a further 2 minutes, until cooked through.
3 Remove from the grill and sprinkle each breast with some of the grated cheese, using about a quarter on each breast. Pop back under the grill for a further 3-5 minutes until the cheese is bubbling and starting to brown.
4 Chill and use as required.

Portions: 4
Suitable for: Phase 2 (fat).
Candida, Hypoglycaemia, Wheat free.

Cajun seasoning
(For chicken, pork, beef, bacon, fish etc.)

This is an all time favourite for so many people. The seasoning can be rubbed on just about anything you like and it lends itself particularly well to food that's grilled or barbq'd. We make big batches and keep the seasoning in a herb jar for everyday use.

½ teaspoon cardamom seeds
1 teaspoon coriander seeds
1 teaspoon cumin seeds
1 teaspoon fennel seeds
1 teaspoon black peppercorns
2 teaspoons dried oregano
1 teaspoon dried basil
1 teaspoon paprika
½ teaspoon chilli powder
½ teaspoon garlic salt.

1 Put the cardamom, coriander, cumin and fennel seeds together with the black peppercorns in a pestle and mortar and crush them well.
2 Transfer the crushed seeds and peppercorns to a mixing bowl and add the remaining ingredients. Mix everything together thoroughly.
3 Rub the mixture into steak, lamb, pork, chicken, fish, aubergine steaks, vegetables and anything else that you would barbecue or grill. Cook the meat, fish or vegetables as you would normally.

Portions: 4
Suitable for: Phase 1 & 2 (can accompany a carb/fat meal). Candida, Hypoglycaemia, Wheat free, Dairy free.

Kebabs - Pork, chicken or beef

450g (1lb) meat, diced (Pork, chicken, beef or a mixture)
4 tablespoons olive oil
2 tablespoons lemon juice
½ teaspoon cumin powder
½ teaspoon cardamom powder
½ teaspoon garam masala
½ teaspoon chilli powder
2 cloves garlic, crushed
1 red & 1 yellow pepper, deseeded and chopped into 2-3 cm squares
(barbecue skewers).

1 Cut the meat into 2-3cm cubes.
2 Mix the oil, lemon juice, spices and garlic.
3 Pour the mixture over the meat, cover and marinate for 60-90 minutes.
4 Alternate the pepper squares with the meat cubes as you slide them onto the skewers.
5 Grill, or barbeque under a high flame, for 10 minutes.

Portions: 4
Suitable for: Phase 1 & 2 (fat).
Candida, Hypoglycaemia, Wheat free, Dairy free.

Coronation chicken wrap

This is a great way to use up any bits of left over chicken, as the appearance of the meat is disguised when it's mixed up with the other ingredients. It's also surprisingly rich and filling.

75g (2.5oz) full fat, Natural Live Yoghurt (Greek style)
1 teaspoon of Dijon mustard
2 dried apricots, chopped (optional)
100g (4oz) precooked chicken (you can use the scrapings off the carcase for this)
Sea salt and freshly ground pepper
2 iceberg lettuce leaves per serving.

1 In a mixing bowl, thoroughly mix the yoghurt, mustard, apricots and chicken and then season with salt and pepper.
2 Take 2 iceberg lettuce leaves and place one inside the other to create a small dish and spoon the mixture into the middle. Then, wrap the lettuce leaves around the chicken and yoghurt mixture and eat with your hands.

Tip: You can leave out the apricots to be strict or just pop a small single dried apricot in the dish. It adds more in taste and texture than it adds in carb content. The Mustard roast chicken recipe on page 20, can help with any mustard queries.

Portions: 1
Suitable for: Phase 2 (fat).
Candida, Hypoglycaemia, Wheat free.

Chicken burgers

This recipe is not what the name suggests. Rather than using ground chicken to make a burger, we'll be using chicken breasts as a replacement for the traditional burger bun.

4 chicken breasts, sliced in half lengthways
8 bacon rashers
2 medium tomatoes, sliced
½ red onion, finely sliced
4 tablespoons Natural Live Yoghurt (NLY) or mayonnaise (see page 84)
Sea salt and freshly ground black pepper.

1 Heat a griddle pan and cook the chicken breast slices for about 5 minutes on each side.
2 While the chicken is cooking, fry or grill the bacon until crispy and prepare the other ingredients.
3 To make the burgers, place a chicken slice on a plate and then build up a layer of NLY/mayonnaise, bacon, tomato and onion and repeat. Season with salt and pepper and top off with another chicken slice.

Tip 1: To make these burgers even more filling, try adding a layer of grated cheese or guacamole instead of the NLY/mayonnaise (this would then make it a Phase 2/3 dish).

Tip 2: Natural Live Yoghurt, rather than mayonnaise, makes this OK for Phase 1 and Candida.

Portions: 4
Suitable for: Phase 1 (can be) & Phase 2 (fat).
Candida (NLY option), Hypoglycaemia, Wheat free, Dairy free (mayo option).

Slow roast pork

Slow roast pork is not only delicious hot, it is also a perfect base for a lunch box meal. If you can resist eating all the crackling hot, then it also adds an interesting texture to your cold meal. Keep some apple sauce back too and spoon a dollop on top of the cold pork.

1kg (2lb) rolled shoulder of pork
1 onion, peeled and sliced into rings.

1 Place the onion rings on a piece of aluminium foil large enough to cover the pork and then place the pork on top of the onions. Wrap the foil around the meat, making sure that it's sealed to keep all the juices in. Cook in a cool oven 135° C, 275° F, Gas 1 for at least 6 hours.

2 Remove from the oven, carefully unwrap the meat and slice off the skin. Re-wrap the joint and leave to stand in a warm place.

3 Put the skin on a tray and pop under a medium grill to crispen. This will take about 10-15 minutes. Resist the temptation to cook it too fast as it will just burn and be ruined.

4 Carve the meat and enjoy hot and chill what remains for your lunch box, carving as required.

Portions: 4-6
Suitable for: Phase 1 & 2 (fat).
Candida, Hypoglycaemia, Wheat free, Dairy free.

Mustard roast ham

Much of the ham that you can buy in supermarkets is preserved with water and sugar, so why not cook your own? It takes little-to-no effort and tastes so good.

1kg (2lb) ham or gammon joint
2 teaspoons Dijon mustard.

1 Spoon the mustard over the ham joint, making sure that it's well covered. Place it on some aluminium foil, large enough to cover the whole joint. Wrap the foil around the meat, making sure that it's sealed to keep all the juices in. Cook in a medium oven, 175° C, 350° F , Gas 4, for about 2 hours.
2 Remove from the oven, open up the foil to expose the meat and return to the oven. Increase the heat to 200° C, 400° F, Gas 6 and roast for a further 30 minutes.
3 Remove from the oven, again, and recover the meat with the foil to rest for about half an hour.
4 Transfer the meat to a dish and chill. Use as required.

Tip: See the mustard roast chicken recipe on page 20 for some thoughts on mustard. Mustard can't be left out of this recipe but you could easily go for the middle cuts from the joint for a Phase 1 meal (avoid the mustard brushed outer layer).

Portions: 4-6
Suitable for: Phase 1 (can be) & 2 (fat).
Candida, Hypoglycaemia, Wheat free, Dairy free.

Scotch eggs

These are traditionally rolled in breadcrumbs to help hold them together but, with a little care, you can make them wheat free and you lose none of the taste.

450g (1lb) minced beef
1 onion, finely chopped
1 clove garlic, crushed
3 teaspoons dried mixed herbs
Few dashes Tabasco
Sea salt and freshly ground pepper
4 small chicken eggs, hard boiled (8 minutes) and shelled.

1 Pre-heat the oven to 200° C, 400° F, Gas 6.
2 Put the minced beef, onion, garlic, herbs, Tabasco, salt and pepper in a mixing bowl and thoroughly mix together.
3 Take a quarter of the mixture and form a thin burger shape. Place a boiled egg onto the mixture and gently fold the minced meat mixture around the egg, pressing firmly so that it holds its shape. Place on a roasting tray and repeat for the other 3 eggs.
4 Pop in the oven and cook for about 40 minutes, until the meat browns. Remove from the oven to cool.
5 Chill and serve as required.

Portions: 4-8 (Note these are quite dense and filling so you may only need ½ of a Scotch egg per lunchbox - especially if you're adding salad and dip selections).
Suitable for: Phase 1 & 2 (fat).
Candida, Hypoglycaemia, Wheat free, Dairy free.

Zingy fish patties

450g (1lb) white fish flaked (cod, hake, Pollack etc will all do)
Juice of half a lemon
1 chilli, deseeded and finely chopped
2 eggs
Freshly ground pepper
Knob of butter for frying.

1 Put the fish, lemon juice and chilli in a mixing bowl and mix together. Leave to stand for 15 minutes for the flavours to infuse.
2 Beat the eggs and add to the bowl. Mix thoroughly until you have a messy looking fish paste, then mix in some freshly ground pepper.
3 Take palm-sized amounts of the paste and mould in your hands to create small fish patties. You should be able to make about 8-10 of them.
4 Heat the butter in a frying pan and gently add the patties. Cook for 3-4 minutes on each side until they are nicely browned.
5 Chill and enjoyed as a snack or add to a lunchbox with your favourite salad and relish.

Portions: 4
Suitable for: Phase 1 & 2 (fat).
Candida, Hypoglycaemia, Wheat free.

Chilli prawns

2 tablespoons olive oil
2 chillies, deseeded & chopped (more if you like food really spicy)
2 cloves of garlic, finely sliced
16 large prawns
Juice of 1 lemon.

1 Heat the olive oil in a frying pan and, when the oil is hot, add the chillies and garlic and fry for 1 minute.
2 Add the prawns and fry for a further 4-5 minutes, turning regularly, until the prawn shells are lightly burnt.
3 Transfer the prawns to a warmed dish and pour the oil from the frying pan over the prawns.
4 Squeeze the juice of the lemon over the prawns, then chill and use as required as a lunch box main or a tasty snack on their own.

Tip, you can use pre-cooked prawns as an option.

Portions: 4
Suitable for: Phase 1 & 2 (fat).
Candida, Hypoglycaemia, Wheat free, Dairy free.

Harissa spiced koftas

450g (1lb) mince lamb
1 small onion, finely chopped
2 teaspoons Harissa paste
Sea salt and freshly ground pepper
(barbecue skewers).

1 Place the lamb, onion and Harissa paste in a mixing bowl and mix thoroughly. Season well with sea salt and freshly ground pepper.
2 Take a small handful of the paste and mould over a wooden skewer, repeat for 7 other skewers, making 8 Koftas. Alternatively, make 8-10 small meatballs.
3 Either fry, grill, roast or barbq the Koftas/meatballs for about 10 minutes (5 mins each side for Koftas or 15 minutes for meatballs).

Tip: Try these with some of the yoghurt dips in the Sauces & Dips section.

Portions: 4
Suitable for: Phase 1 & 2 (fat).
Candida, Hypoglycaemia, Wheat free, Dairy free.

Meatzas

If you've previously enjoyed delicious, thin crust pizzas, laden with bubbling melted cheese, herbs, peppers and tomatoes but now abstain from wheat, you should try a Meatza.

Meatzas basically replace the floury pizza base with a delicious ground meat base, which can be jazzed up with onions, herbs and spices. Top them off with your favourite pizza topping and you have a very tasty, and nutritious, pizza alternative.

You can cook up a Meatza for an evening meal and then chill what's left for use in your lunchbox over the next couple of days. Once cooked, it will keep for up to 5 days in your fridge.

Here's our basic recipe, which you can adapt to suit your own preferences.

For the base:
450g (1lb) mince beef
Olive oil for cooking
1 large onion, very finely chopped
1 clove garlic, crushed
1 egg
1 teaspoon dried oregano
1 teaspoon dried basil
½ teaspoon dried fennel
Sea salt and freshly ground pepper.

1 Pre-heat the oven to 200° C, 400° F, Gas 6.
2 Gently fry the onion and garlic in a generous amount of olive oil. Do this very slowly - they should be lightly caramelised when done.
3 In a mixing bowl, add the minced meat, fried onion, herbs and egg and mix thoroughly. Then, pat into the base of a baking dish so that the whole base is covered.

4 Cook in the oven for 20-30 mins until the mixture is a dark brown.

5 Pour off some of the excess fat from the baked base and allow to cool for about 10 minutes.

6 For the simplest of toppings, cover with cheese, peppers, tomatoes and any other ingredients that you fancy and place back in the oven. Cook for a further 15 minutes until the cheese is bubbling. For other toppings, we have some suggestions on the following pages.

Base variations:

Try different minced meats, like chicken, pork, turkey or lamb and different herbs and spice combinations. For example, Lamb with Rosemary or Oregano; Turkey with oregano and cumin; or a mixed beef and pork mince with onion and garlic.

Portions: 4-6
The base is suitable for: Phase 1 & 2 (fat).
Candida, Hypoglycaemia, Wheat free, Dairy free.

Once you add cheese to your toppings, you're no longer Phase 1 and dairy free.

Meatza toppings

Quattro stagioni

200g (7oz) of tinned tomatoes (chopped)
4 artichoke hearts (tinned are fine)
Handful of black olives
150g (5oz) sliced mushrooms
50g (2oz) finely chopped ham
1 Mozzarella (approx. 100g (3.5oz))
Drizzle of olive oil.

1 Spread the chopped tomatoes over the meatza base.
2 Arrange the other four toppings (artichoke hearts, olives, mushrooms, ham), along with some Mozzarella in each of the four quarters of the meatza base.
3 Drizzle some olive oil over the topping and pop under a hot grill for about 10 minutes until the Mozzarella is bubbling.
4 This is perfect chilled for your lunchbox with one or two of the salads.

Margherita

200g (7oz) of tinned tomatoes (chopped)
1 clove garlic, finely chopped
300g (10.5oz) Mozzarella, chopped into small chunks
100g (3.5oz) grated Parmesan or Pecorino
Handful of fresh basil leaves, cut into strips
2 tablespoons olive oil.

1 Spread the chopped tomatoes over the Meatza base.

2 Arrange the remaining ingredients evenly over the base of your Meatza.

3 Drizzle some olive oil over the topping and pop under a hot grill for about 10 minutes until the cheese melts.

4 This is perfect chilled for your lunchbox with one or two of the salads.

Tex-Mex

200g (7oz) of tinned tomatoes (chopped)
100g (3.5oz) cheddar cheese, grated
2 tablespoons grated parmesan cheese
1 teaspoon chopped jalapeno pepper
4 spring onions, chopped
2 cloves garlic, minced
1 avocado, chopped
100g (3.5oz) sour cream
2 tablespoons chopped fresh coriander.

1 Spread the chopped tomatoes over the meatza base.

2 Mix the grated cheddar and Parmesan together and then sprinkle over the tomatoes.

3 Sprinkle the peppers, onions, garlic and avocado evenly on top of the cheese and then place under a hot grill until the cheese is bubbling.

4 Remove from the grill and spoon the sour cream on top.

5 Sprinkle with coriander and serve.

Tip: You can leave out the avocado if you don't want to mix at all, but this is still pretty much a fat meal.

Lunchbox 'Eggza' (v)

Our lunchbox Eggza is our meat-free alternative to our Meatza base, which will allow you to enjoy all your regular 'pizza' favourites using the humble egg. The bases are quick and easy to make and you can then add your favourite 'pizza' toppings.

Basic 'Eggza' Base:
4 eggs
1½ tablespoons almond flour
50g (2oz) grated parmesan, or other hard cheese alternative
Sea salt and freshly ground pepper.
Butter for frying.

1 Whisk the eggs in a mixing bowl and then stir in all the other ingredients.
2 Melt the butter in a frying pan and pour in the mixture, making sure the pan is evenly covered. Cook on a low heat for about 15-20 minutes until the mixture is set.
3 Turn out onto a baking dish and create your favourite topping. If the topping needs cooking, pop it under the grill for a few minutes.

Tip: For the carb conscious, almond flour has about 1.5g of carbohydrate per tablespoon, so you've only got a couple of grams of carbohydrate in this whole recipe.

Portions: 4
Suitable for: Phase 2 (fat).
Candida, Hypoglycaemia, Wheat free.

Homemade pâté

Liver is one of nature's super foods but many people unfortunately find the texture unpalatable. Pâté, therefore, is a great way to get healthy liver into your diet in a delicious dish. Once made, the pâté should keep for a week in a cold fridge and you can eat it as a snack (delicious on celery), with a salad and one guest even had it for breakfast with their bacon and egg!

1 teaspoon butter
1 large onion, chopped
450g (1lb) lambs liver, chopped
2 bacon rashers, chopped
Butter for cooking
Salt & pepper – plenty
½ teaspoon dried Italian herbs
50g (2oz) double cream.

1 Heat the butter in a frying pan and lightly fry the onion. Set it aside.
2 Fry the liver & bacon in this pan until browned.
3 Return the onions to the pan and stir well together. Add the salt & pepper and ½ the herbs.
4 Put the mixture in a mixing bowl and cool for 10 minutes.
5 Add the cream and hand blend until the substance forms a coarse paste.
6 Place the pâté in small pots, or one serving dish, as desired.
7 Add a knob of butter to the frying pan and the rest of the herbs. Melt and pour on top of the pâté for an authentic and delicious finish.

Portions: 4
Suitable for: Phase 2 (fat).
Candida, Hypoglycaemia, Wheat free.

Chicken liver parfait

This is another pâté recipe that is so easy to make. You can whizz it up in 15 minutes and enjoy it for the rest of the week.

1 teaspoon butter
½ onion, finely chopped
1 clove garlic, crushed
250g (9oz) chicken livers
½ teaspoon dried thyme
2 tablespoons brandy (optional)
50g (2oz) butter.

1 Heat the butter in a frying pan and lightly fry the onion and garlic. Transfer the onion and garlic to a mixing bowl and then quickly fry the chicken livers in the same pan. Turn the livers frequently and cook for about 5-6 minutes. Do not overcook - the livers should still be pink inside.
2 Add the livers to the onion and garlic and add the thyme, brandy and butter. With a hand blender, blend the mixture until you have a smooth paste. Then spoon it into a suitably sized pot/bowl.
3 Melt a little butter, about 10g/ ½ oz in the frying pan and pour over the parfait in the pot (there's no need to heat the pan, there should be enough residual heat to melt the butter).

Tip: The brandy is for the dinner party version and connoisseurs. Leave it out for Phase 1.

Portions: 4-6
Suitable for: Phase 1 (can be) & 2 (fat).
Candida, Hypoglycaemia, Wheat free.

Cheese & bacon muffins

Makes 12 cups:
12 slices bacon
8 eggs
50g (2oz) grated cheddar cheese
pinch of salt
freshly ground black pepper.

1 Preheat oven to 175° C, 350° F, Gas 4.
2 Lightly coat a tray with 12 muffin holes with a little olive oil (or use a 6 hole tray for larger cups). Wrap each piece of bacon inside each muffin cup.
3 Whip the eggs, salt, pepper and cheese with a fork and fill each bacon lined muffin cup ¾ of the way with the egg mixture.
4 Bake for 30-35 minutes, until the egg cups are golden brown and don't jiggle. Use a knife to scoop them out of the tins.
5 Allow to cool and serve with one of your favourite salad options.
6 For a variant, mix in some finely chopped red pepper with the eggs in step 3.

Tip: Leave out the cheese for Phase 1 bacon & egg muffins.

Portions: 6
Suitable for: Phase 1 (can be) & Phase 2 (fat).
Candida, Hypoglycaemia, Wheat free, Dairy free (can be).

Loaded bacon strips

Bacon isn't just for breakfast. These loaded bacon strips are delicious served as the main part of a lunchbox or as a healthy and tasty snack to keep in the fridge, just in case.

8 slices bacon
Homemade Guacamole (page 88)
Homemade tomato salsa (page 80)
Freshly ground black pepper.

1 Grill the bacon under a hot grill for 3-4 minutes each side, until the fat is nicely browned. Transfer to a plate to cool.
2 Spoon the Guacamole onto the bacon strips, pressing it down slightly so that it stays in place.
3 Spoon some homemade salsa on top and finish with some freshly ground pepper.

Tip: You can 'load with just salsa if you don't want to mix at all, but this is still pretty much a fat meal.

Portions: 4
Suitable for: Phase 1 (with just the salsa) & Phase 2/3 (with the Guacamole) (fat).
Candida, Hypoglycaemia, Wheat free, Dairy free.

Egg mayonnaise (v)

This is another classic dish, made 'Harcombe friendly' by swapping out a few ingredients. We suggest you batch cook the eggs and then make the 'mayo' fresh as required.

4 tablespoons Natural Live Yoghurt
1 teaspoon Dijon mustard
Salt and freshly ground pepper
4 eggs, hardboiled.

1 Mix the yoghurt, mustard, salt and pepper in a bowl.
2 Peel the eggs and roughly chop them into the bowl with the yoghurt mix.
3 Give the whole lot a good stir with a fork and then use as required.

Portions: 4
Suitable for: Phase 2 (fat)
Candida, Hypoglycaemia, Wheat free.

Omelette strips (v)

This is a great way to use up any leftover meat or veg that may be in your fridge while providing a delicious lunch option that you can toss into your lunchbox. It's basically an omelette, which you allow to cool and then slice up into strips to top your salad with.

Large knob of butter
Handful of any leftover meat or veg (e.g. chicken, beef, broccoli, cauliflower, beans, onions etc.)
4 eggs
Salt and freshly ground pepper.

1 Lightly fry the leftovers in the butter for 3-5 minutes until warmed through.
2 Break the eggs into a bowl, give them a good whisk with a fork, season with salt and pepper then pour them into the frying pan.
3 Cook for a further 5 minutes, stirring occasionally during the first minute until the whole mixture is cooked through then fold out onto a plate and leave to cool.
4 Chill in a fridge until required then slice into 2cm wide strips to top your salad.

Portions: 2
Suitable for: Phase 1 & 2 (fat).
Candida, Hypoglycaemia, Wheat free.

Oopsies (v)

Oopsies are extremely versatile and a great alternative to bread rolls. Once cooked, they can be used as a gluten free hotdog or hamburger bun or as a base for some whipped cream and berries (leave out the rice flour for non-savoury options).

3 eggs
A generous pinch of sea salt
100g (3.5oz) cream cheese
½ tablespoon rice flour (optional – will make the oopsies more bread like).

1 Pre-heat the oven to 150° C, 300° F , Gas 2.
2 Separate the eggs whites in one bowl and yolks in another.
3 Whisk the egg whites together with the salt until they are very stiff.
4 Mix the egg yolks and the cream cheese and then stir in the rice flour.
5 Tip the egg whites into the yolk mix and fold the two mixtures together.
6 Divide into 6 to 8 oopsies on a baking tray and bake for about 25 minutes, until a golden colour.

Tip: If you're in Phase 3, try mixing in a handful of mixed seeds before cooking to give a crunchier texture.

Portions: 2-4
Suitable for: Phase 2 (fat).
Candida, Hypoglycaemia, Wheat free.

Frittata (v)

Frittata's are an endlessly versatile dish that are equally as delicious as a snack or a main dish for a meal. You can serve them warm or cold and they are a perfect pre-prepare option for lunchboxes.

Large knob of butter
1 large red pepper, diced
50g (2oz) fresh spinach
6 eggs
100g (3.5oz) feta cheese
Some freshly ground black pepper.

1 Melt the butter in a heavy frying pan and lightly fry the diced pepper for about a minute, then cover with the fresh spinach.
2 Whisk the eggs and pour them over the spinach. Cook on a low heat for about 5 minutes and then crumble the feta cheese into the mixture. Cook for a further 15 minutes, or until the whole mixture is set.
3 Turn out (upside down) onto a large plate so that the nicely brown underside is facing up.
4 Serve a slice immediately and/or chill for the lunch box.

Options: Try broccoli and tuna; cheese and mushroom; cheese and tomato; bacon and onion, for starters.

Portions: 2-4
Suitable for: Phase 2 (fat).
Candida (if no mushrooms), Hypoglycaemia, Wheat free.

Spicy chick pea patties (v)

225g (8oz) tin chick peas, drained and rinsed
25g (1oz) butter
1 medium onion, finely chopped
1 teaspoon ground cumin
1 teaspoon paprika
450g (1lb) tomatoes, finely chopped
100g (3.5oz) Cheddar cheese, grated
Sea salt and pepper.

1 Put half the chick peas in a bowl and blend with a hand blender, using a little water, if needed.
2 Melt the butter in a frying pan and lightly cook the onion for 5 minutes, until transparent. Then stir in the cumin and paprika and the remaining chick peas and cook for a further 2 minutes, stirring frequently. Add the tomatoes and blended chick peas.
3 Reduce the heat and simmer for 10 minutes to thicken the mixture.
4 Remove from the heat and stir in the cheese and season to taste and allow to cool. Then take a handful of the mixture and make into a small pattie and repeat until all the mixture is used up.
5 Lightly fry the patties on both sides in a little butter until lightly browned. Then chill and use as required.

Portions: 4
Suitable for: Phase 3 (mix) (Always better to mix with real food than cheat with fake food).
Candida, Hypoglycaemia, Wheat free.

Wheat-free flans (v)

Like Frittatas, flans are endlessly versatile dishes and this delicious wheat free version means that you can enjoy it without having those wheat belly moments.

150g (5oz) white rice flour
1 teaspoon rosemary, chopped
1 teaspoon sea salt
100g (3.5oz) butter, chilled and cut into small pieces
50ml (2oz) cold water
2 tablespoons butter or olive oil.

For the Topping:
2 teaspoons butter
1 large onion, peeled and finely sliced
75g (2.5oz) Emmental cheese, sliced
2 large tomatoes, sliced.

1 In a bowl, mix the white rice flour, rosemary, and salt.
2 Add the butter and mix with a fork until no large pieces of butter remain. The mixture should now look like a crumble. Add the water and continue mixing until you have a doughy mixture.
3 Lightly grease a flan dish and, one-tablespoon piece of dough at a time, press into the bottom of the flan dish, covering the dish evenly. Lightly cover the dish with plastic wrap and freeze for 30 minutes.
4 Preheat the oven to 190° C, 375° F, Gas 5.
5 For the topping: Melt the butter in a frying pan and add the onion and fry for about 20 minutes until lightly brown. Stir frequently.
6 Remove the base from the freezer and cover the top with butter or oil. Pop in the oven and bake the base for about 30 minutes, until lightly brown. Remove from the oven.
7 Cover the flan base with the sliced Emmental and spoon

the onions evenly over cheese. Finish with the sliced tomatoes. Drizzle lightly with olive oil.

8 Increase the oven temperature to 220° C, 425° F, Gas 7 and bake for a further 20 minutes until the tomatoes soften. Remove from the oven and allow to cool on a wire rack.

9 Serve as required.

Portions: 4-6
Suitable for: Phase 3 (mix).
Candida, Hypoglycaemia, Wheat free.

Why not try out some of these alternatives toppings, or create your own favourite: Courgette, pepper & Mozzarella; Roasted tomatoes & Feta; Asparagus & Cheddar cheese.

Courgette, pepper & Mozzarella

1 buffalo Mozzarella, sliced
1 courgette, finely sliced
1 red pepper, finely sliced.

1 Slice the Mozzarella thin enough so that the slices completely cover the flan base (recipe page 48).
2 Arrange the courgette and red pepper slices over the Mozzarella so that they evenly cover the base.
3 Cook in the oven at 200° C, 400° F, Gas 6 for a further 30 minutes.

Suitable for: Phase 2 (fat) for this topping.
Candida, Hypoglycaemia, Wheat free.

Roasted tomatoes & Feta

4 large tomatoes, quartered
2 tablespoons olive oil
100g (2oz) feta cheese, crumbled.

1 Place the quartered tomatoes on a baking tray and drizzle over the olive oil. Pop in a preheated oven at 200° C, 400° F, Gas 6 for 30 minutes, until the tomatoes start to brown.
2 Sprinkle the crumbled feta over the flan base (recipe page 48) and then evenly cover with the roasted tomatoes, making an attractive pattern.
3 Cook in the oven at 200° C, 400° F, Gas 6 for a further 30 minutes.

For a spicier alternative, replace the roasted tomatoes with some chilli roast tomatoes (page 62).

Suitable for: Phase 2 (fat) for this topping.
Candida, Hypoglycaemia, Wheat free.

Asparagus & Cheddar cheese

300g (10.5oz) asparagus
2 eggs
50g (2oz) cheddar cheese, grated
200ml (7oz) double cream
Sea salt and freshly ground pepper.

1 Remove the woody end of the asparagus and drop the tips
into boiling water and cook for 3 minutes. Drain and rinse
with cold water. Then chop them into 3cm, lengths and
arrange onto the flan base (recipe page 48).
2 Whisk the eggs in a mixing bowl and stir in the cream and
cheddar. Season well and then pour the mixture over the
asparagus.
3 Cook in the oven at 200° C, 400° F, Gas 6 for a further 30
minutes.

Suitable for: Phase 2 (fat) for this topping.
Candida, Hypoglycaemia, Wheat free.

The toppings suggested for the wheat free flan base can
also be used as topping options on our Lunchbox Eggza
(page 40).

Lentil & buckwheat biscuits (v)

100g (3.5oz) buckwheat
2 tablespoons olive oil
1 onion, finely chopped
1 carrot, grated
175g (6oz) red lentils
1 litre (1.5pints) vegetable stock
2 teaspoons chopped parsley
Sea salt and pepper.

1 Preheat the oven to 200° C, 400° F, Gas 6.
2 Under a hot grill, toast the dry buckwheat grains for about 5 minutes until golden brown.
3 Heat the oil in a frying pan and lightly fry the onion and carrot for about 5 minutes until the onion is transparent.
4 Add the toasted buckwheat, along with all the other ingredients, and pour the stock into the pan. Bring quickly to the boil and then reduce and simmer for about 30 minutes until all the liquid is absorbed by the ingredients.
5 Press the mixture into a greased baking dish and score with a knife to make biscuit sized chunks. Bake for 30 minutes until the top is nicely brown.
6 Allow to cool then turn out onto a plate and break into 'biscuits' along the score lines.

Portions: 4-6
Suitable for: Phase 2 (carb).
Candida, Hypoglycaemia, Wheat free (despite the name, buckwheat is not wheat).

Lentil & cheese slab (v)

Like the spicy chick pea patties this does mix pulses and cheese, but these are great options for vegetarians for a healthy and filling lunch. Mix cheating is always better than sandwiches.

225g (8oz) red lentils
450ml (1pint) water
1 large onion, finely chopped
25g (1oz) butter
100g (3.5oz) cheddar cheese, grated
1 teaspoon dried mixed herbs
1 egg, beaten
1 tablespoon rice flour (optional)
Salt and pepper to season.

1 Preheat the oven to 200° C, 400° F, Gas 6.
2 Put the lentils and water in a saucepan, bring to the boil, then reduce and simmer for about 30 minutes, until the lentils are soft. Drain and transfer to a mixing bowl.
3 Fry the onion with the butter for about 5 minutes until transparent, then add this to the lentils.
4 Add all the other ingredients to the mixing bowl and mix thoroughly. Then press the mixture into a greased flan dish or sandwich tin and bake in a moderate-hot oven 200° C, 400° F, Gas 6 for 30 minutes, or until the top is nicely brown.
5 Allow to cool then transfer to a plate, if using a flan dish, or slice from the sandwich tin.

Portions: 4
Suitable for: Phase 3 (mix).
Candida, Hypoglycaemia, Wheat free.

Carrot, parsnip, celeriac & mixed seed bake (v)

This is a great alternative to nut roast - using seeds and root vegetables instead of nuts and rice.

1kg (2lb) total weight of grated carrot, parsnip and celeriac - equal quantities
½ red onion, finely chopped
½ teaspoon chopped rosemary
100g (3.5oz) mixed seeds (pumpkin, sunflower, sesame etc)
1 egg, beaten
1 tablespoon rice flour
freshly ground pepper and generous pinch of sea salt.

1 Preheat the oven to 175° C, 350° F, Gas 4.
2 Put the grated carrot, parsnip and celeriac in a large mixing bowl along with the onion, rosemary and mixed seeds and mix thoroughly.
3 In a separate bowl, whisk the eggs and rice flour then pour over the mixture in the first bowl and mix thoroughly with a fork.
4 Spoon the mixture into a loaf dish (or shallow baking dish) and squeeze down so that the whole mixture is compacted.
5 Roast in the oven until the top starts to brown.

Portions: 4
Suitable for: Phase 3 (mix).
Candida, Hypoglycaemia (if you are very carb sensitive, this quantity of root vegetables may be best avoided), Wheat free.

Chewy fruit bars (v)

Due to the high level of fruit and nuts, these bars are not strictly 'Harcombe friendly'. However, when compared to other cereal bar alternatives, these are a much better option for busy people on the go. If you're a sales rep, for example, and you really can't store meat and salads safely in the car 'till lunch time, these bars are far better than the meal deal at the service stations.

100g (3.5oz) dried apricots, chopped
100ml (3.5oz) orange juice
1 teaspoon orange rind, grated
50g (2oz) desiccated coconut
50g (2oz) mixed nuts, chopped
100g (3.5oz) ground almonds
50g (2oz) dried fruit
50g (2oz) puffed rice cereal.

1 Put the apricots, orange juice and rind in a small pan, quickly bring to the boil then reduce and simmer for 5 minutes.
2 Put the desiccated coconut and chopped nuts on a baking tray and lightly toast for 2-3 minutes until they start to lightly brown.
3 Put the ground almonds, dried fruit and puffed rice cereal in a mixing bowl and blitz for a few seconds with a hand blender. Then stir in all the other ingredients.
4 Pour the ingredients into a lightly greased shallow biscuit tin, pressing the mixture down flat. Cut them into equal sized 'bars', probably around a dozen, then leave on a cooling rack to dry out and solidify.

Portions: 10-12
Suitable for: Phase 3 (mix).
Candida, Wheat free.

Nut roast (v)

Strictly a Phase 3 dish, as it mixes fats and carbs in reasonable quantities, but this is a very satiating loaf to keep hunger at bay when you're out and about.

175g (6oz) brown rice (dry weight)
600ml (21oz) of vegetable stock
2 small onions, finely chopped
1 clove garlic, finely chopped
4 mushrooms, finely chopped
1 stick celery, finely chopped
2 tablespoons olive oil
175g (6oz) mixed nuts, chopped (hazelnuts, cashews, almonds & brazils work really well)
1 sprig fresh rosemary
1 sprig fresh thyme
(or ½ teaspoon of each herb dried if you can't get fresh)
Salt & ground black pepper
1 egg (optional)
1 apple, (cooking or eating).

1 Preheat the oven to 200° C, 400° F, Gas 6.
2 Part cook the brown rice in the vegetable stock (cook for half the recommended time).
3 Drain the rice through a sieve and put it in a mixing bowl and leave it to one side.
4 Stir-fry the vegetables in the olive oil. Then add them to the rice.
5 Add the chopped nuts to the mixing bowl with the rice & vegetables.
6 Add in the rosemary, thyme, salt & pepper.
7 Crack the egg into a small bowl and beat with a fork until mixed in.
8 Add the egg to everything else (without the egg the mixture doesn't bind and will be crumbly but this doesn't

affect the taste).

9 Put half the mixture into a loaf (glass) oven dish and press it down well into the dish.

10 Core & slice the apple on top of the mixture until it makes an apple layer. Put the rest of the mixture on top (pressing it down well again) so that you have made an apple sandwich.

11 Cover the loaf dish with tin foil.

12 Bake for 30-45 minutes, or until the top of the roast is golden.

TIP 1: Substitute peppers for the mushrooms, or just leave out the mushrooms, for this dish to be suitable for Candida.

Tip 2: This is perfect for vegetarians to bake at the weekend and then five lunches are sorted – just vary the salads and dips.

Portions: 4-6
Suitable for: Phase 3 (mix).
Candida, Hypoglycaemia, Wheat free, Dairy free.

Chapter 5
Salads

There is a lot more to salads than a few wilted lettuce leaves that you used to get as garnish with your pub meal. With a little creativity, salads can make any lunch an exciting and exotic mix of flavours, packed with nutrients to help keep you alert through to your next meal. We've listed some of our favourites, which can be made and stored usually for up to five days at any time of the year (check the use-by date, but always do the 'sniff & taste' test).

In this chapter:
Chilli roast tomatoes (v)
Coleslaw with yoghurt (v)
Celery & apple with yoghurt (v)
Waldorf salad (v)
Creamy beetroot salad (v)
Watercress & beetroot salad (v)
Watercress & tomato salad (v)
Mixed leaf salad (v)
Greek salad (v)
Citrus salad (v)
Mixed pepper & red onion salad (v)
Beetroot with fresh mint (v)
Tomato, bean & basil salad (v)
Herb grilled tomatoes (v)
Pear & blue cheese salad (v)
Butternut squash wedges (v)

Chilli roast tomatoes (v)

400g (14oz) cherry tomatoes
4 tablespoons olive oil
1-2 teaspoons chilli flakes.

1 Preheat the oven to 175° C, 350° F, Gas 4.
2 Put the tomatoes in a roasting dish and drizzle the olive oil over them.
3 Sprinkle the chilli flakes over the tomatoes and pop in the pre-heated oven and roast for 30 minutes, until the tomatoes start to brown.
4 Chill and serve as required.

Tip: The oil mixed with the tomato juices is sweet and hot and is a deliciously simple dressing for a green salad.

Suitable for: Phase 1 & 2 (can accompany a carb/fat meal). Candida, Hypoglycaemia, Wheat free, Dairy free.

Coleslaw with yoghurt (v)

250g (9oz) Natural live yoghurt (NLY)
1 large teaspoon of Dijon mustard
Freshly ground pepper
Big pinch of sea salt
½ red onion, finely chopped.
1 large carrot, grated,
¼ celeriac, grated and equal in volume to the large carrot
¼ red cabbage, finely chopped.

For a red cabbage free version (low FODMAP* alternative),
replace the vegetables as follows:
1 red onion, finely chopped.
2 large carrots, grated,
½ celeriac, grated and equal in volume to the large carrot.

1 Put the NLY, mustard, salt and pepper in a large mixing
bowl and stir to a smooth consistency.
2 Add all the chopped and grated vegetables and stir well.
3 Serve as desired.

Suitable for: Phase 2 (fat).
Candida, Hypoglycaemia, Wheat free.

* FODMAPs stands for **F**ermentable, **O**ligo-, **D**i-, **M**ono-saccharides and
Polyols. They comprise fructose, lactose, fructo- and galacto-
oligosaccharides (fructans and galactans), and polyols (such as sorbitol,
mannitol, xylitol and maltitol) that are poorly absorbed in the small
intestine. People aware of FODMAPS avoid some foods because it helps
with Irritable Bowel Syndrome and tummy discomfort.

Celery & apple with yoghurt (v)

If you're in Phase 3, or don't worry about a healthy mix, this is tastier with normal (full fat) Natural Live Yoghurt. However, we've advised low-fat NLY here because the apples make this a carb meal.

In 2 large apples there are approximately 60g of carbohydrate, of which almost 50g is sugar (the rest being fibre). A handy reminder of just how sugary fruit is. Do try this recipe though - it's a meal in itself.

250g (9oz) low-fat Natural Live Yoghurt (NLY)
Juice of half a lemon
Big pinch of sea salt
Freshly ground pepper
2 large apples, cored and thinly sliced
4 sticks of celery, finely chopped.

1 Put the NLY, lemon juice, salt and pepper in a large mixing bowl and stir to a smooth consistency.
2 Add all the sliced apple and chopped celery and stir well.
3 Serve as desired.

Suitable for: Phase 2 (carb).
Candida, Hypoglycaemia, Wheat free.

Waldorf salad (v)

The classic Waldorf salad has celery, apple, nuts and mayonnaise. This would be a mix with the carb of the apple, the fat of the mayo and the natural mix of the nuts. To lessen the mix, we go for red pepper instead of the apple. It's just as crunchy and colourful, but we now have a mostly fat meal, with just a dash of nut mixing.

4 celery sticks, finely sliced
50g (2oz) walnuts
1 red pepper, deseeded and diced
150g (5oz) mayonnaise (see recipe page 84)
Sea salt and freshly ground pepper.

1 Put all the ingredients into a large mixing bowl and mix thoroughly.
2 Chill and serve as required.

Options:
1. Replace the mayonnaise with Natural Live Yoghurt (NLY) for a tangier option and to avoid the vinegar in the mayo if you're very Candida sensitive.
2. Add a couple of diced dried apricots for a bit of sweetness and a bit of mixing if desired.

Suitable for: Phase 2 (fat).
Candida (if the mayonnaise is replaced with NLY),
Hypoglycaemia, Wheat free, Dairy free (if mayo, not NLY).

Creamy beetroot salad (v)

250g (9oz) beetroot, grated
250g (9oz) parsnips, grated
3 teaspoons chopped parsley
150g (5oz) Natural Live Yoghurt
2 tablespoons cider or white wine vinegar
Sea salt and freshly ground pepper.

1 Add the grated beetroot and parsnips to a large mixing bowl and then add all the other ingredients and mix thoroughly.
2 Chill and serve as required.

Options:
1. Replace the parsnips with carrots.
2. Leave out the vinegar for a great Phase 1 coleslaw alternative.

Suitable for: Phase 1 (can be) & Phase 2 (fat).
Candida (without the vinegar), Hypoglycaemia, Wheat free.

Watercress & beetroot salad (v)

100g (3.5oz) watercress, roughly chopped
4 medium beetroot, cooked, peeled and quartered
2 tablespoons extra virgin olive oil
Sea salt and freshly ground pepper.

1 Mix the watercress and beetroot in a bowl and then pour over the olive oil.
2 Season and serve as required.

Suitable for: Phase 1 & 2 (can accompany a carb/fat meal).
Candida, Hypoglycaemia, Wheat free, Dairy free.

Watercress & tomato salad (v)

100g (3.5oz) watercress, roughly chopped
¼ cucumber, diced
250g (9oz) tomatoes, diced
3 teaspoons fresh mint, chopped
2 tablespoons olive oil or classic French dressing (see page 85)
Sea salt and freshly ground pepper.

1 Mix all the salad ingredients in a bowl and then toss with sufficient dressing to cover the salad.
2 Season and serve as required.

Tip: Choose the olive oil option to be suitable for Phase 1.

Suitable for: Phase 1 (can be) & Phase 2 (can accompany a carb/fat meal).
Candida (with olive oil, not the French dressing), Hypoglycaemia, Wheat free, Dairy free.

Mixed leaf salad (v)

This is hardly a recipe, more a reminder that, sometimes, the simplest of dishes are the tastiest and should not be forgotten. You can get pre-packed bags of mixed leaves from the supermarket, which are pre-washed (bleached) or you can make your own from simple leaves (much tastier and far more nutritious).

Approximately 400g (14oz) of mixed leaves – e.g. Cos, Romaine, little gems, round head, radicchio, spinach, rocket, watercress etc
2 tablespoons olive oil or classic French dressing (page 85)
Sea salt and freshly ground pepper.

1 Rinse the leaves in cold running water and spin dry in a salad spinner. Chop up all the various leaves into roughly the same size pieces and put in a large mixing bowl.
2 Drizzle over the olive oil or French dressing and toss the leaves until they are all nicely covered by the oil/dressing.
3 Season with salt and pepper. Give the leaves a final toss and serve.

Tip1: Choose the olive oil option to be suitable for Phase 1.
Tip2: This is absolutely delicious topped with the Celery & apple with yoghurt salad (page 64).

Suitable for: Phase 1 (can be) & 2 (can accompany a carb/fat meal).
Candida (with olive oil, not the French dressing), Hypoglycaemia, Wheat free, Dairy free.

Greek salad (v)

200g (7oz) iceberg lettuce, shredded or chopped
75g (2.5oz) cucumber, diced
4 medium tomatoes, diced
1 small red onion, thinly sliced
150g (6oz) feta cheese
1 tablespoon freshly chopped basil
50ml (2oz) classic French dressing (page 85)
Sea salt and freshly ground pepper.

1 Add all the ingredients to a large mixing bowl and toss until the leaves are well covered with dressing.
2 Season to taste and serve as required.

Tip: Use olive oil instead of French dressing to be suitable for Candida.

Suitable for: Phase 2 (fat).
Candida (can be), Hypoglycaemia, Wheat free.

Citrus salad (v)

This is a classic example of a real food mix that is so worth it. The taste in this salad is incredible. You'll really feel like you've had a meal and - if it gets you through to dinner with no snacking - it's done its job.

2 oranges, peeled, pith removed and cut into segments
4 spring onions, chopped
225g (8oz) sweetcorn
100g (3.5oz) cashew, walnut or mixed nuts
1 teaspoon sesame seeds (roasted if time permits)
1 teaspoon ground ginger
1 teaspoon Tamari soya sauce
50ml (2oz) French dressing or olive oil
Sea salt and freshly ground pepper.

1 Add all the ingredients to a large mixing bowl and toss until the leaves are well covered with dressing.
2 Season to taste and serve as required.

Tip: Use olive oil instead of French dressing to be suitable for Candida.

Suitable for: Phase 3 (mix).
Candida (can be), Hypoglycaemia, Wheat free, Dairy free.

Mixed pepper & red onion salad (v)

50g (2oz) olive oil
2 cloves garlic, thinly sliced
1 large red pepper, deseeded and sliced
1 large yellow pepper, deseeded and sliced
1 large green pepper, deseeded and sliced
1 red onion, thinly sliced
1 tablespoon white wine vinegar
Sea salt and freshly ground pepper.

1 Heat the oil in a frying pan and add the garlic, fry for about a minute until it just turns brown.
2 Reduce the heat, add the peppers and onion and cook for about 10 minutes, stirring frequently, until they just begin to soften.
3 Transfer the mixture to a mixing bowl, pour over the white wine vinegar and give the whole lot a good stir.
4 Season, chill and serve as required.

Tip: Leave out the vinegar for Phase 1.

Suitable for: Phase 1 (can be) & Phase 2 (can accompany a carb/fat meal).
Candida (without the vinegar), Hypoglycaemia, Wheat free, Dairy free.

Beetroot with fresh mint (v)

6 medium beetroot, cooked, sliced or diced
2 tablespoons balsamic vinegar
Handful of fresh mint, chopped
2 tablespoons olive oil
Sea salt and freshly ground pepper.

1 Add all the ingredients to a large mixing bowl and mix
thoroughly with a fork until the ingredients are well mixed
together.
2 Chill and use as required.

Suitable for: Phase 2 (can accompany a carb/fat meal).
Candida, Hypoglycaemia, Wheat free, Dairy free.

Tomato, bean & basil salad (v)

5 tablespoons olive oil
15g (½oz) fresh basil or coriander leaves, roughly chopped
300g (10.5oz) cherry tomatoes, halved
400g (14oz) tin of mixed beans, drained and rinsed
Sea salt and freshly ground pepper.

1 Heat the olive oil in a pan and lightly fry the basil leaves
for about a minute, until they start to change colour.
2 Add the tomatoes and beans to a mixing bowl, season
with salt and pepper and pour over the basil and oil and stir
well.
3 Chill and serve as required.

Suitable for: Phase 2 (carb).
Candida, Hypoglycaemia, Wheat free, Dairy free.

Herb grilled tomatoes (v)

Dr Kaayla Daniel calls vegetables "a delivery mechanism for butter"! This recipe certainly is.

These are equally delicious hot or cold – make plenty – some for the lunch box and some to fry with eggs for breakfast.

6 medium tomatoes
2 teaspoons dried mixed herbs
25g (1oz) butter.

1 Chop the top off the tomatoes and gently slash the flesh with a small sharp knife.
2 Sprinkle each tomato with dried mixed herbs and top with a small knob of butter.
3 Grill under a medium grill until the butter melts and the herbs start to brown.

Suitable for: Phase 1 & 2 (can accompany a carb/fat meal). Candida, Hypoglycaemia, Wheat free.

Pear & blue cheese salad (v)

This can double as a dinner party starter, as well as a 5* lunch box option. It's a mix because of the fruit with the cheese dressing. We think of pears as a lower sugar fruit, but a small pear still has 23g of carbohydrate, of which approximately 15g is sugar. This really is a meal in itself, however, even though it's in the salad section.

4 pears, quartered and cored
100g (3.5oz) blue cheese dressing/dip (page 89)
1 tablespoon balsamic vinegar
3 tablespoons olive oil.

1 Place the pears in a mixing bowl and spoon over the blue cheese dressing and mix until the pears are nicely covered by the dressing.
2 Mix the olive oil and vinegar together in a cup and then drizzle over the pear and blue cheese.
3 Chill and use as required.

Suitable for: Phase 3 (mix).
Hypoglycaemia, Wheat free.

Butternut squash wedges (v)

1 butternut squash, quartered and deseeded
3 tablespoons olive oil
1 tablespoon fresh herbs, finely chopped.

1 Preheat the oven to 200° C, 400° F, Gas 6.
2 Place the butternut squash quarters on a roasting dish and drizzle the olive oil over them. Roast in a preheated oven for 30 minutes then remove from the oven.
3 Sprinkle the squash with the herbs and pop back in the oven for a further 15 minutes until the flesh is soft and the edges begin to brown.
4 Chill and use as required.

These wedges are delicious on their own, topped with raw tomato salsa (page 80) and a green salad.

Suitable for: Phase 1 & 2 (can accompany a carb/fat meal).
Candida, Hypoglycaemia, Wheat free, Dairy free.

Chapter 6
Sauces & Dips

Sauces and dips are great with crudités as an appetiser at dinner parties and they also give a fantastic boost to any packed lunch. We've taken some classic dips and made them 'Harcombe friendly' and have included a few others that we've created or come across on our travels. We usually make a few in advance, so that we have some variety throughout the week.

In this chapter:
Raw tomato salsa (v)
Lanzarote mojo sauces (v)
Yoghurt dips & sauces (v)
Basic mayonnaise (v)
Classic French dressing (v)
Aioli (v)
Hummus (v)
Guacamole (v)
Blue cheese dressing/dip (v)
Infused oils (v)
Yellow pepper & coriander relish (v)

Raw tomato salsa (v)

There's nothing quite like a good tomato relish to add to cold meats and this one is so simple, there's no excuse for not always having a small pot in the fridge.

450g (1lb) ripe tomatoes
A few healthy dashes of Tabasco sauce
1 tablespoon wine vinegar
1 clove garlic, crushed
½ red onion, finely chopped
Sea salt and freshly ground pepper
2 tablespoons fresh basil, chopped
100g (3.5oz) olive oil.

Liquidise the tomatoes with a food processor or blender and then add all the other ingredients. Whisk with a fork and serve as a side relish.

Suitable for: Phase 2 (can accompany a carb/fat meal). Candida, Hypoglycaemia, Wheat free, Dairy free.

Lanzarote mojo sauces (v)

We recently visited Lanzarote for the first time and we loved it. The climate was delightful and the food was deliciously fresh and simple. These sauces were served at every meal and you'll understand why, as they add a burst of taste and colour to just about any dish.

Red version:

2 large, sweet red peppers, deseeded and sliced
5-8, fresh red chillies, deseeded and sliced
50g (2oz) olive oil
Juice of 1 lemon
Sea salt.

1 Cook the peppers and chillies in a little salted water for 3-4 minutes, until they start to soften.
2 Drain and puree the pepper and chilli in a blender, then stir in the olive oil and lemon juice.
3 Mix in a good pinch of sea salt and chill.
4 Will keep up to a week in a fridge.

Suitable for: Phase 1 & 2 (can accompany a carb/fat meal). Candida, Hypoglycaemia, Wheat free, Dairy free.

Green version:

3 cloves garlic, crushed
Sea salt
1 teaspoon cumin, ground
Handful of fresh coriander or parsley, chopped
10ml (½oz) white wine vinegar
50g (2oz) olive oil.

1 Place the garlic into a mixing bowl and crush it with some sea salt (it helps to chop the garlic first).
2 Once it's finely crushed, add the cumin and coriander, then mix in the white wine vinegar.
3 Finally, slowly pour in the olive oil, whisking as you add it, until you have a lovely smooth green sauce.

Suitable for: Phase 2 (can accompany a carb/fat meal). Hypoglycaemia, Wheat free, Dairy free.

Yoghurt dips & sauces (v)

Natural Live Yoghurt (NLY) makes a wonderful base for a sauce, dip or salad dressing. Our first one uses fresh mint, which gives a deliciously fresh taste. If you like this one, try some of the other suggestions below.

250g (9oz) Natural Live Yoghurt
Handful of fresh mint, chopped
Sea salt and freshly ground pepper.

1 Put all the ingredients in a mixing bowl and mix thoroughly.
2 Chill for a few hours and then use as required.
3 This will keep up to five days in an airtight container in a fridge and the longer you keep it, the stronger the mint flavour.

Variations (replace the mint with):
1. 2 teaspoons of paprika; Or
2. Lots of freshly ground black pepper; Or
3. The juice of 2 fresh chilli's, crushed with a garlic crusher; Or
4. Handful of fresh coriander or basil, chopped; Or
5. ¼ cucumber, deseeded and chopped into small chunks.

Suitable for: Phase 1 & 2 (fat).
Candida, Hypoglycaemia, Wheat free.

Basic mayonnaise (v)

2 eggs, at room temperature
Juice of half a lemon
1 tablespoon wine vinegar
Sea salt and pepper
200ml (7oz) extra virgin olive oil

1 Break the eggs into a food processor and add all the other ingredients, except the oil.
2 Blend on high for about 30 seconds until the eggs are foaming. Turn the speed down to half and pour in the oil slowly and evenly until you end up with a consistent paste.
3 Will keep up to 5 days in an airtight container in a fridge.

Suitable for: Phase 2 (fat).
Candida, Hypoglycaemia, Wheat free, Dairy free.

Classic French dressing (v)

3 tablespoons white wine vinegar
2 teaspoons Dijon mustard
5 tablespoons olive oil
Sea salt and freshly ground black pepper.

1 Put the white wine vinegar and Dijon mustard in a bowl or mug, and whisk with a fork until completely combined.
2 Slowly add the olive oil, whisking all the time, until you have a smooth emulsion.
3 Season well with sea salt and pepper.

This dressing should have quite a bite to it, but if it's too mild for your taste, add some more mustard or vinegar.
    This recipe also works with other mustards and vinegars. Try sherry or cider vinegar and wholegrain mustard.

Suitable for: Phase 2 (fat).
Hypoglycaemia, Wheat free, Dairy free.

Aioli (v)

4 cloves garlic
1 egg yolk
100g (3.5oz) olive oil
Juice of half a lemon
Sea salt and freshly ground pepper.

Put all the ingredients, except the olive oil, into a food processor, turn on, blend for a few seconds and then slowly pour in the oil until you have a beautiful, thick sauce.

Suitable for: Phase 1 & 2 (fat).
Candida, Hypoglycaemia, Wheat free, Dairy free.

Hummus (v)

Go for low-fat Natural Live Yoghurt (NLY) if you want to avoid mixing. Enjoy the regular NLY if you're fine with a bit of mixing. This makes a perfect vegetarian carb lunch with a couple of oat biscuits.

250g (9oz) tin of chickpeas, drained and rinsed
1 clove garlic, finely chopped
Juice of half a lemon
2 tablespoons olive oil
4 tablespoons low-fat Natural Live Yoghurt
Sea salt and freshly ground pepper
Chopped parsley to garnish (optional).

1 Drain the tinned chickpeas and place them in a saucepan. Cover with water, bring to the boil and then simmer for about 20 minutes until they soften. Then drain and allow to cool.
2 Put the oil, lemon juice, garlic, yoghurt and chick peas into a mixing bowl and give them a few quick blasts with a hand blender (or put the ingredients in a food processor and blast for a few seconds).
3 Season with salt and pepper and give a final quick stir with a spoon.
4 Transfer to a dish and sprinkle with chopped parsley.
5 Chill and use as required.

Suitable for: Phase 2 (carb).
Candida, Hypoglycaemia, Wheat free.

Guacamole (v)

In a 100g portion of avocado there are 15g of fat and 9g of carbohydrate. Avocados are, therefore, higher in fat than carb but they are a bit of a mix food. Have them in moderation in Phase 2 and with a fat meal when you do have them.

3 avocados
Juice of 1 lemon/lime (lime is traditionally used with guacamole, but lemons are more easily available)
1 small shallot, finely diced
Sea salt and freshly ground pepper.

1 In a medium bowl, combine the diced shallot, salt, and lemon/lime juice. Set aside for 10 minutes.
2 Pit and peel the avocados. Take half of the flesh and mash it in a bowl with a fork.
3 Pour the lemon/lime mixture into the bowl and combine with the mashed avocado.
4 Dice the remainder of the avocado flesh into 3/4-inch cubes and gently incorporate into the mixture in the bowl.
5 Add freshly ground pepper and a good pinch of sea salt.

Suitable for: Phase 2/3 (fat).
Candida, Hypoglycaemia, Wheat free, Dairy free.

Blue cheese dressing/dip (v)

100g (3.5oz) butter, softened
100g (3.5oz) blue cheese like Roquefort
Freshly ground black pepper
1 tablespoon olive oil.

1 Whisk the butter, cheese, olive oil and pepper into a smooth paste and use immediately.
2 This will keep in a fridge for a week but you will need to soften the dressing before use (else it will just be like a hard lump of cheese!)

Suitable for: Phase 2 (fat).
Hypoglycaemia, Wheat free.

Infused oils (v)

The principle here is simple. Take about 250ml olive oil and heat it gently in a saucepan with the chosen ingredients for 15-20 minutes. Allow to cool then strain the oil into a glass bottle with a small additional amount of the ingredient and leave it to infuse for 2-3 weeks. Then use as required as an alternative to plain olive oil. You'll be amazed at the difference this simple little change will make to your salads. Here are some of our favourites to get you started.

Rosemary
Heat the oil with a handful of rosemary twigs. Allow to cool, then transfer to a glass bottle. Add a few sprigs of rosemary and seal for 2-3 weeks then use as required. Delicious on all meats, meatzas, eggzas and flans.

Chilli
Heat 8-10 whole small fresh or dried chillies, different colours make the infusion more attractive. Allow to cool, then transfer to a glass bottle. Add a few fresh/dried chillies and seal for 2-3 weeks then use as required. This is great for adding a kick to your cooking and salads.

Peppercorns
Heat 2 tablespoons mixed peppercorns (the Bristol blend has different colours) with the oil, then allow to cool before transferring to a glass bottle. Add a few peppercorns to the bottle, then seal for 2-3 weeks. Delicious on all salad greens.

Yellow pepper & coriander relish (v)

2 tablespoons sesame oil for cooking
2 large yellow peppers, seeded and diced
½ medium red onion, very finely sliced
1 large red chilli, deseeded and thinly sliced
Handful fresh coriander, chopped
Sea salt.

1 Heat the oil in a frying pan and lightly fry the peppers for about 5 minutes, until they start to turn brown.
2 Add the red onion and cook for a further minute.
3 Transfer the peppers to a mixing bowl and add the coriander, sliced chilli and salt.
4 Stir well with a fork then chill before use.

Suitable for: Phase 1 & 2 (can accompany a carb/fat meal).
Candida, Hypoglycaemia, Wheat free, Dairy free.

Appendices

A – Foods you can eat

We sometimes hear people say that eating real food is too restrictive for modern day living and that there is not enough variety. We find this quite ironic given how restrictive the typical modern human's diet really is, being made up of predominantly, wheat, corn and sugar.

If you ever thought eating real food would limit your food choices, here's a starter list to think about and try.

When you combine the range of cuts of meat available (our ancestors would have eaten ALL the animal, not just the posh- cuts) with vegetables, herbs, fruits and so many different cooking methods, you can see the range of dishes that are available to us when we eat real food.

When we think of the abundance of options open to us, we can celebrate what we can have and not miss the rubbish that we can't.

Meats:
Beef, Buffalo, Chicken, Duck, Goat, Goose, Grouse, Lamb, Pheasant, Pigeon, Pork, Quail, Rabbit, Turkey, Venison (Plus Alligator, Bison, Crocodile, Elk, Emu, Frog, Kangaroo, Moose, Ostrich, Snails and Squirrel if you're going to be really adventurous!)

Fish and Seafood:
Barracuda, Cod, Catfish, Char, Carp, Herring, Salmon, Trout, Grayling, Shark, Barramundi, Bass, Sea-bass, Mackerel, Tuna, Whiting, Bream, Turbot, Halibut, Coley, Eel, Dab, Dorado, Grouper, Emperor, Perch, Flatfish, Flounder, Haddock, Hake, Halibut, John Dory, Kingfish, Lemon sole, Sole, Ling, Mahi-mahi, Monkfish, Mullet, Parrotfish, Perch, Pike, Plaice, Pollock, Red Snapper, Roach, Sardine, Snapper, Sole, Swordfish, Whitebait, Octopus, Squid, Lobster, Shrimp,

Mussels, Clams (and dozens of other seafoods).

Vegetables:
Artichokes, Asparagus, Aubergine, Bamboo, Beetroot, Broccoli, Brussels sprouts, Burdock, Cabbage (many varieties), Carrots, Cauliflower, Celeriac, Celery, Chard, Chicory, Courgettes, Cress, Cucumbers, Dandelion nettles, Endive, Fennel, Garlic, Kale, Kohlrabi, Lamb's lettuce, Leeks, Lettuce, Okra, Olives, Onions, Parsnips, Peppers, Radish, Salsify, Scallions, Shallots, Sorrel, Spinach, Squash (dozens of varieties), Tomatoes, Water chestnuts.

Herbs & Spices:
Allspice, Anise, Basil (many varieties) Bay Leaf, Black Mustard, Caraway, Cardamom, Carob, Cayenne pepper, Celery seed, Chervil, Chicory, Chilli Pepper, Chives, Cinnamon, Clove, Coriander, Cumin, Curry, Dill, Elderflower, Fennel, Fenugreek, Garlic, Ginger, Horseradish, Jasmine, Lavender, Lemongrass, Licorice, Mace, Marjoram, Mint, Mustard, Nutmeg, Oregano, Paprika, Parsley, Pepper, Peppermint, Rosemary, Saffron, Sage, Sorel, Spearmint, Star anise, Tarragon, Thyme, Turmeric, Vanilla, Wasabi, Watercress.

Fruits (in moderation):
Apple, Apricot, Avocado, Banana, Bilberry, Blackberry, Blackcurrant, Blueberry, Cherry, Damson, Date, Elderberry, Fig, Gooseberry, Grape, Grapefruit, Guava, Kiwi fruit, Kumquat, Lemon, Lime, Lychee, Mango, Melon (many kinds), Nectarine, Orange, Papaya, Peach, Pear, Pineapple, Pomegranate, Raspberry, Redcurrant, Satsuma, Star fruit, Strawberry.

B - Phase 1 Summary

1) **Eat when you need to.** It is best to get into the habit of eating three main meals a day with in between meal snacks only if you are genuinely hungry.

2) **Eat as much as you need** of anything on the 'allowed' list.

3) **Do not eat anything that is not on the allowed list** during Phase 1 – no fruit, no other grains, no milk, cheese or any other dairy products.

Phase 1 Allowed list

Vegetables & Salads. Alfalfa, Artichoke, Asparagus, Aubergine, Bamboo shoots, Bean sprouts, Beetroot, Broccoli, Brussels sprouts, Bok choy, Cabbage (any), Carrots, Cauliflower, Celeriac, Celery, Chicory, Chillies (any), Courgettes, Cucumber, Dandelion, Endive, Fennel , Garlic, Green beans, Kale, Leeks, Lettuce (any), Mange tout, Marrow, Mustard greens, Okra, Onions, Parsnip, Peas, Peppers (any), Pumpkin, Radish, Rocket, Salsify, Shallots, Sorrel, Spinach, Spring onions, Squashes, Swiss chard, Swede, Turnip, Watercress, Water chestnuts.

Herbs & Spices. Basil, Bay leaves, Caraway, Cardamom, Chervil, Chives, Cinnamon, Cloves, Coriander, Cumin, Dill, Ginger, Marjoram, Mint, Nutmeg, Oregano, Paprika, Parsley, Pepper, Rosemary, Saffron, Sage, Salt, Tarragon, Thyme, Turmeric.

White Fish. Cod, Haddock, Halibut, Plaice, Turbot, Whiting.

Seafood. Clams, Crab, Lobster, Mussels, Oysters, Prawns,

Winkles.

Oily Fish. Anchovies, Mackerel, Pilchards, Salmon, Tuna, Trout.

White Meat & Birds. Chicken, Duck, Goose, Guinea Fowl, Pheasant, Quail, Rabbit, Turkey.

Red Meat. Bacon, Beef, Gammon, Ham, Lamb, Pork, Veal, Venison.

Other. Eggs, Natural Live (Bio) Yoghurt, Tofu.

Misc. Butter, Olives, Olive oil, Tomatoes.

Drinks. Water, Herbal teas, Decaf tea & coffee.

The only food limited in quantity is brown rice/quinoa/plain oats of which you can have 50g dry weight or 150g if you are vegetarian.

If you are allergic or intolerant to any 'allowed' foods, clearly avoid these.

C - Phase 2 Summary

Phase 2 has just three rules. They are your secret to being fit, not fat, and staying there. The three rules are:

1) Don't eat processed foods;

2) Don't eat fats and carbs at the same meal;

3) Don't eat any foods that you currently crave.

The super handy summary for Phase 2 is on the next page.

Phase 2 Allowed list

FAT MEALS	CARB MEALS
Any unprocessed meat – bacon, beef, chicken, duck, goose, guinea fowl, ham, lamb, pheasant, pork, quail, rabbit, turkey, veal, venison	All **Fruit**
	Whole-grains – brown rice, brown pasta, brown rice pasta, couscous, 100% wholemeal bread, quinoa, millet etc.
Any unprocessed fish – cod, haddock, halibut, mackerel, plaice, pilchards, salmon, seafood, trout, tuna, whiting etc. Includes tinned fish in only oil, salt and/or water	**Wholemeal cereal –** porridge oats, Brown rice cereal, Shredded Wheat®, other sugar-free cereal
Eggs – Chicken, duck etc.	**Beans & Pulses** – lentils, broad beans, kidney beans, chickpeas etc.
Dairy Products – Cheese, milk, butter, cream, yoghurt (ideally Natural Live Yoghurt)	Baked **Potatoes** in their skins

EAT WITH EITHER A FAT OR A CARB MEAL
Salads – alfalfa, bean sprouts, beetroot, celery, chicory, cress, cucumber, endive, all types of lettuce, radish, rocket, spring onions etc.
Vegetables – artichoke, asparagus, aubergine, bamboo shoots, broccoli, Brussels sprouts, cabbage, carrot, cauliflower, celeriac, chillies, courgettes, garlic, green beans, kale, leek, mange tout, marrow, okra, onions, parsnip, peas, peppers (any colour), pumpkin, salsify, shallots, spinach, squashes, swede, turnip, water chestnuts etc.
Tofu/Quorn – Vegetarian protein alternatives
Certain **Fruits** – olives, tomatoes & berries
Low-fat dairy products – milk, cottage cheese & yoghurt
Herbs, Spices & Seasoning – basil, chives, coriander, cumin, dill, fennel, mint, oregano, paprika, parsley, pepper, rosemary, sage, salt, thyme etc. Olive oil for cooking.

Other books by Zoë Harcombe:

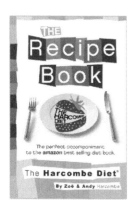

The Harcombe Diet:
The Recipe Book

Real food; great taste; optimal health – that's what The Harcombe Diet® is all about and here's how to do it. With over 100 recipes for Phase 1, another 100 for Phase 2 and some seriously special Phase 3 cheats, this is the ultimate diet-recipe book. If you want to eat well, lose weight and gain health – this is a must for your kitchen shelf.

ISBN 978-1-907797-07-1

The Harcombe Diet:
Stop Counting Calories
& Start Losing Weight

You've tried every diet under the sun. You've lost weight and put it back on. The more you diet, the more you crave food. You've given up hope of being slim. This book explains why. Count calories & end up a food addict. Stop Counting Calories & Start Losing Weight!

ISBN 978-1-907797-11-8

Copies available on www.theharcombediet.com

Other books by Zoë Harcombe:

The Harcombe Diet for Men:
No More Mr Fat Guy

Men want to lose weight too - fast - and they won't go hungry. They want steak, pasta, cheese and the good things in life, including wine. They'll exercise if they want to; they won't count calories and they want all the answers in just a few pages... So here it is - The Harcombe Diet® for men!

ISBN 978-1-907797-12-5

Why do you overeat? When all you want is to be slim

This book will explain Why do you overeat? when all you want is to be slim. It will tell you about the three common medical conditions, which are causing insatiable food cravings. It will give you the perfect diet to overcome these three conditions and so to end food addiction and overeating forever.

ISBN 978-1-907797-24-8

Copies available on www.theharcombediet.com

Other books by Zoë Harcombe:

The Obesity Epidemic
What caused it?
How can we stop it?

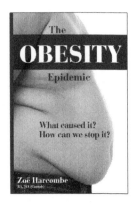

"The Obesity Epidemic is the most comprehensive demolition job on the arrogance and ignorance of the health profession I have ever read". *Barry Groves. Author Trick and Treat: How 'healthy eating' is making us ill.*

ISBN 978-1-907797-00-2

The Harcombe Diet®
Lunch box recipes

**Find out more about Zoë and/or
The Harcombe Diet® at:**

www.zoeharcombe.com

www.theharcombediet.com

www.theharcombedietclub.com

Index

W

Waldorf salad 65
Watercress & beetroot salad 67
Watercress & tomato salad 68
Wheat free flans 50

Y

Yellow pepper & coriander relish 91
Yoghurt dips & sauces 83

Z

Zingy fish patties 33